CLIPCHAMP VIDEO EDITOR MADE EASY

Creating Memories Like a Pro

By James Bernstein

Printed in the United States of America

Bernstein, James
Clipchamp Video Editor Made Easy
Part of the Productivity Apps Made Easy series

For more information on reproducing sections of this book or sales of this book,
go to **www.madeeasybookseries.com**

Contents

Introduction

Thanks to the invention of the smartphone, we can now record all the special moments of our lives, and even the not so special ones as I am sure you have seen if you have ever gone on a website such as YouTube or have an Instagram account! Of course smartphones are not the only device you can use to record video and many people still use video cameras to record things such as weddings, graduations and other special events.

One thing that is fairly common with people who record videos is that many times the video ends up being shown with all the footage that really doesn't need to be seen, or the video ends up not being seen at all because the person doesn't have the means to edit out all the unwanted footage to make a watchable video.

This is where using video editing software comes into play. When you have an easy way to edit and enhance your footage and create something that others would enjoy watching, it makes the editing process fun and rewarding. Plus if you do it right, you can end up with a professional looking video that might even make you some money, or at least get you a bunch of views if you post it online!

Microsoft has included video editing software with Windows for many years which used to be called Windows Movie Maker. Then they updated the software and called it Windows Video Editor. But for Windows 11, they have completely changed the video editing software that comes built into Windows. This new video editing software is called Clipchamp and can also be used with Windows 10 after a quick download.

The goal of this book is to get you comfortable using the Clipchamp video editor without confusing and irritating you at the same time. I find that if you explain things like someone is a beginner, even if they are not, it makes that topic much easier to understand, and that is the way this book was written—so that *anyone* can make sense of the content without feeling lost.

This book will cover a wide variety of topics such as the Clipchamp interface, editing and cropping your video clips, adding audio and images, using effects, exporting and uploading your videos and so on. By the time you are done reading this book, you will be surprised at how easy it is to make some very professional looking videos using this free software.

So, on that note, let's import some videos and work towards winning that Oscar!

Chapter 1 – Getting Started

Since Clipchamp might be new to you or maybe you were used to using the older Windows Video Editor app, I will begin this book by discussing how to open Clipchamp and install it if necessary. I will also be covering what you get with the free version and what additional features you can get if you decide to sign up for a subscription to the software. I will then go over the basic Clipchamp interface so you can get an idea of what you can do with the app.

Free vs. Subscription Versions

Clipchamp is free to use but like with most free apps, there is a pay for version that will give you additional features for a price. For most people, the free version will work just fine and if you were to use a video editing app that you had to pay for, there are many other choices to consider so be sure to shop around if you decide to go the paid subscription route.

Figure 1.1 shows the difference between the free and paid versions and as you can see, you get a decent number of features with the free version and if you don't need the brand kit option or the backup feature then you should be just fine with the free version. You will also notice that you get premium audio, image and video stock as well as premium filters and effects with the pay for version but whether or not this is worth it depends on how much you would use these features. Keep in mind that you do get these features with the free version, but they are just more limited.

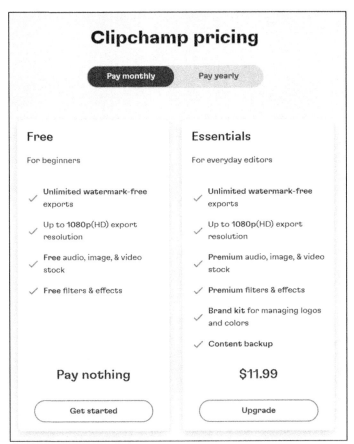

Figure 1.1

As you can see, if you wanted to use the extra features that come with Clipchamp, you would need to pay $11.99 a month to do so. If you pay for a year in advance, then it will cost you $119.99 for the year.

Downloading and Installing Clipchamp
If you are using Windows 11 on your PC then there is a good chance that you already have Clipchamp installed and it's just a matter of finding the app on your computer. Since Microsoft now owns Clipchamp, they have decided to integrate it with their operating system. You can either check your program list or do a search for Clipchamp and open it that way.

If you don't have Clipchamp installed or are running Windows 10, you can go to the Microsoft Store app that you can find in Windows and then do a search for Clipchamp. You will know you found the right version when you see the purple clapperboard icon and the distributor says Microsoft Corporation.

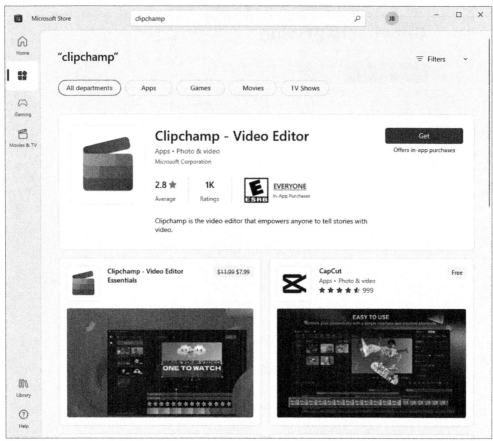

Figure 1.2

To install the app simply click on the Get button and wait for it to download and install. When it's complete you can open the app from the Microsoft Store itself or find the icon in your app listing within Windows.

When you open Clipchamp the first time, you will most likely be asked to sign in with your Microsoft or another account (figure 1.3). You may also be asked what types of videos you will be creating as well (figure 1.4). It's not too important that you answer this accurately or even at all because your answer will be used simply for suggested content that might match the video you are creating.

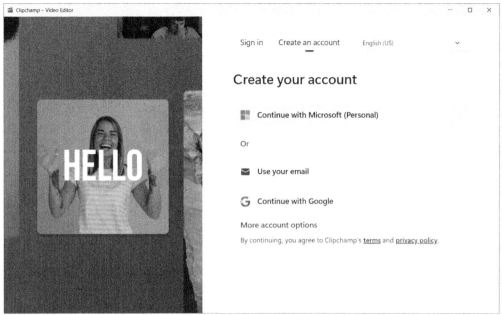

Figure 1.3

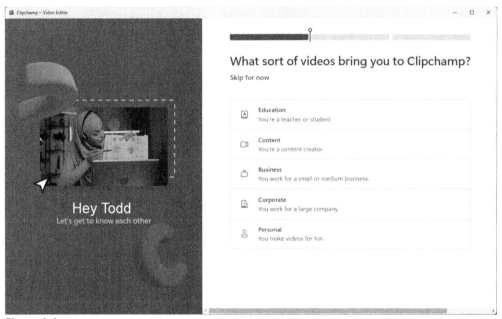

Figure 1.4

The Clipchamp Interface

Once you get the app installed and get signed in, you will be presented with the main Clipchamp interface which looks pretty simple when you first open it (figure 1.5). On the left side of the window, you will have your main sections such as your home page and any folders you might create to help keep your videos organized.

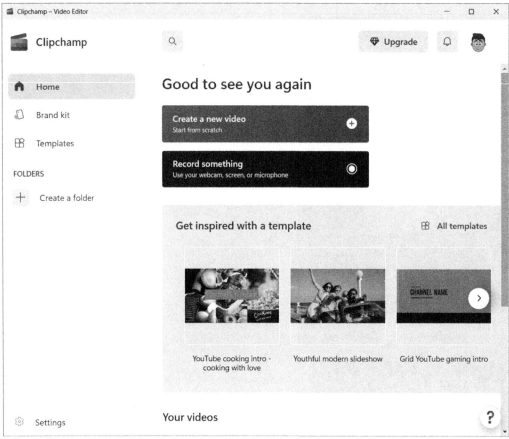

Figure 1.5

If you are using the free version of Clipchamp, you will not be able to do anything with the *Brand kit* section. The Brand kit is used as a place to store things such as your brand or company logo, standard fonts and default colors to help you keep your videos consistent if you are trying to keep them looking similar in their design.

Templates are used as a way to add preconfigured sounds, colors, transitions and so on to your videos so you can use them as a starting point when creating your movies. Clipchamp comes with many built in templates and you can also search for the style that suits your video theme.

Once you start a new video, you will be taken to the main video editor interface as seen in figure 1.6. The left side of the screen contains options to do things such as add music, text and images while the right side of the screen has options that you will use to edit your video such as adjusting the volume, colors and speed of the video.

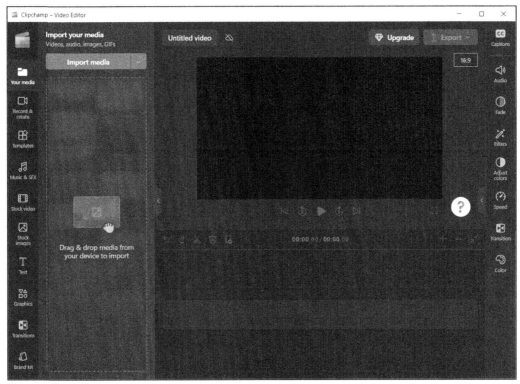

Figure 1.6

The middle section of the app is where your video preview screen is located and below that is the timeline that is used to edit the video if you need to crop out sections or add effects and graphics etc. Since I don't have any video footage loaded, my preview area and timeline and blank.

App vs. Web Version
If you don't want to install the Clipchamp app on your computer or are using a device, you can then log in and access Clipchamp from their website located at: https://app.clipchamp.com/

The Clipchamp website app is currently only supported on the Microsoft Edge and Google Chrome web browsers. As you can see in figures 1.7 and 1.8, the website version of Clipchamp looks virtually identical to the Windows app.

Chapter 1 – Getting Started

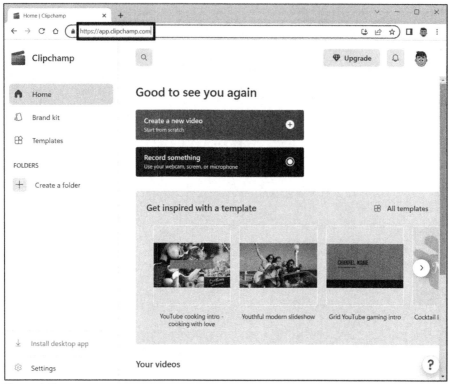

Figure 1.7

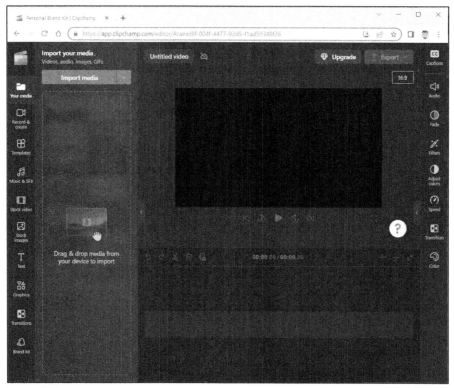

Figure 1.8

Clipchamp is a progressive web app (PWA) which means it's a website that acts like an application so that is why the installed app and online web app look identical to each other.

Depending on your internet speed, you might run into performance issues using the editor on the website vs. on your desktop. Plus if you create a movie using the app and add media (video files etc.), they will not be there when you edit the movie on the website unless you upload them there as well unless you use the content backup service that comes with the premium subscription plan. This also applies if you add media to the website copy of the video project.

Chapter 2 – Importing Videos a New Project

In order to edit videos to create your final award winning film, you will first need to import your existing video or videos into Clipchamp so you can start editing them. There are two main ways you can go about doing this. You can import an existing video clip from your computer, phone or cloud (online) storage location. The other option is to record a video on the spot and then use that clip for your movie.

Supported Video, Audio and Image File Types
The type of video file you will be editing will be based on the device you are recording the video with. For example, an Android smartphone will not use the same video format as an iPhone and your digital camera may also use a different type. Fortunately, Clipchamp supports most standard video, audio and image formats.

You will most likely be adding audio such as music files to your projects as well as possibly some still images so it's good to know which types of files are supported by Clipchamp to ensure that they will work with your video.

Here is a listing of the supported file types that can be used with Clipchamp.

Video files
- .mp4
- .mov
- .webm
- .avi
- .divx
- .flv
- .3gp
- .wvm
- .vob
- .dcm
- .mkv

Audio files
- .mp3
- .wav
- .ogg

Image files
- .jpeg
- .jpg
- .png
- .tiff
- .bmp
- .gif

Creating a New Project

Once you have Clipchamp installed and running, you will need to create a new project in order to start editing your videos, assuming you don't already have a project in progress.

From the Home page, you will have an option to create a new video or record a video on the spot to use for your project. For the most part, you will be using the first option because even if you want to record a video with your webcam for example, it might take you a few tries to get it right and then you can save that video and use it in your project using the create a new video method.

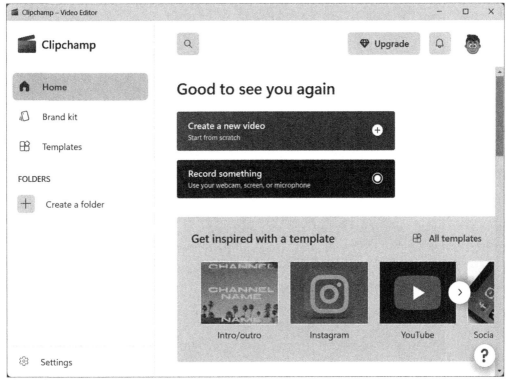

Figure 2.1

I will be discussing the options you have if you do decide you want to use the record something option later in this chapter but for now, I will be using the *create a new video* option.

Once you start a project, you will be presented with a "blank canvas" like you saw back in chapter 1. You will not be able to do much here until you add a video to your project. You might want to change the title from *Untitled video* so a name that is related to your project, especially if you plan to have multiple videos in the works at the same time.

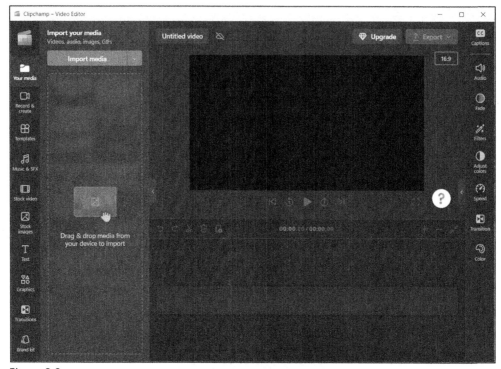

Figure 2.2

Importing Existing Videos From Your Computer

Now that I know what type of method I will be using to create my masterpiece, I will need to import some video clips so I can start editing them. I will be creating a mountain biking video with a combination of first person on the bike shots and other videos taken of other riders from a distance.

I will be working with some rather large files, and you might notice some lagging or stuttering in your preview if your computer's hardware is not up to par with video editing requirements. At a minimum, your computer should have at least 8GB of RAM and a fairly modern processor. You should be ok with the built in video card that most desktop PCs come with but if you have a gaming video card for example, it will really help out with the performance. Just keep in mind that just because you experience slow performance while editing your video that it won't come out that way after you export it.

To see the file size and video size of your videos, you can right click on them and then choose *Properties* (Windows PCs). From the *General* tab you can see the size of the file and from the *Details* tab you can see the length as well as the dimensions of the file. Figure 2.3 shows a 2.3GB video file that is about 6 minutes long and has a resolution of 2704 x 1520. It also shows it was recorded at 60 fps (frames per second).

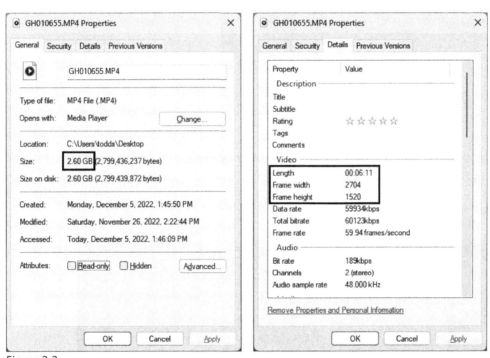

Figure 2.3

To import my first video into my project, I will click on the *Import media* button. Then I will browse to the location on my computer where I have my video files that were imported from my camera. Then I will choose the video I want to import and click on the Open button. I can also drag and drop my video files right into the Clipchamp editor.

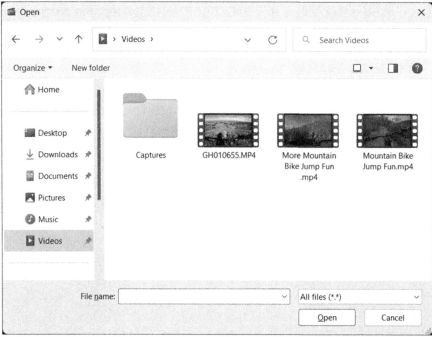

Figure 2.4

Depending on the size of your video, it may take a bit of time to process it before it's ready to be used in Clipchamp.

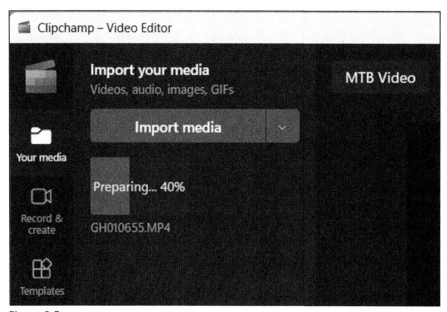

Figure 2.5

Figure 2.6 shows my video media pane after adding my videos. As you can see, the media pane allows you to view just your videos, audio or images or you can also view everything in one place (All section).

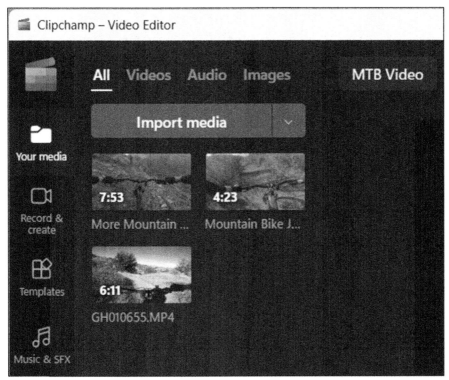

Figure 2.6

You can also click the dropdown next to the Insert media button and add videos from your online\cloud storage locations such as OneDrive, Google Drive, Google Photos and Dropbox.

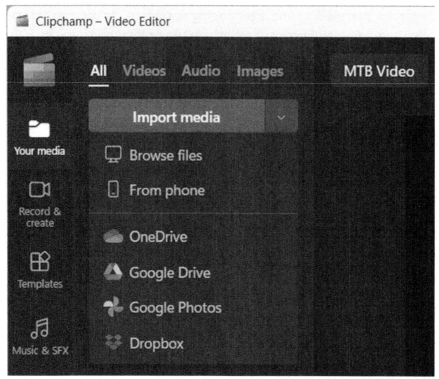

Figure 2.7

The *From phone* option can be used to upload files from your phone right to your online Clipchamp account but they will be used for your online video projects rather than the projects that you use with the Clipchamp app on your local computer.

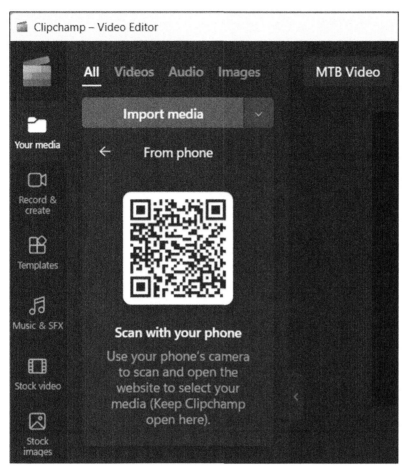

Figure 2.8

Recording a Video for Your Project

If you need to record a video on the spot to add to a new project, you can do so very easily. Or you can also record the video, save it to your computer and then add it using the method I previously discussed.

If you click on *Record and create* button, you will be able to record a video and then add it directly into your project. You have four options when using this method. You can capture what you are doing on your computer along with your webcam, capture your camera only, your screen only, or create a text to speech recording.

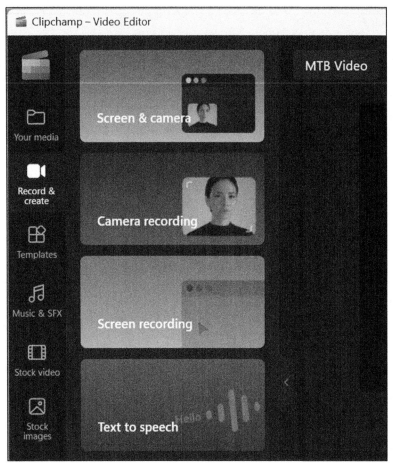

Figure 2.9

The *text to speech* recording option will let you type in some text and then choose a voice that you want to use to have your text read. Then you can add this audio clip to your project and use it for narration over your video footage.

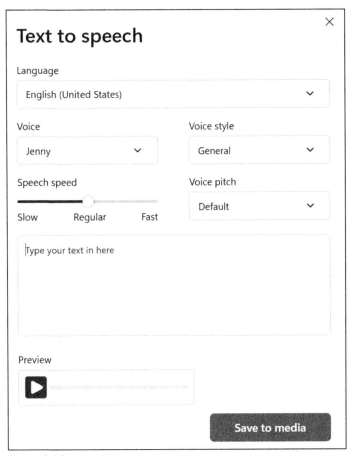

Figure 2.10

Whichever of these options you choose, the footage will then appear in your media along with any other media you added before.

Downloading Videos From Your Camera\Smartphone

Since most of us use our smartphones as our cameras, it makes sense that we would want to be able to transfer videos from our phones to our computers. There are two ways you can go about this. You can copy them over which means you will have the same photos and videos on your phone and computer. Or you can move them to your computer and remove them from your phone which is what you will need to do if your goal is to free up space on your phone.

The first step in the process is to connect the USB cable that came with your phone to the normal charging port on your phone, and then to a free USB port on your computer. I will be using an Android based smartphone for my demonstration so if you have an iPhone, the process will look a little different.

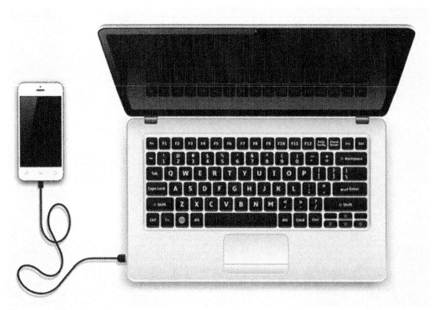

Figure 2.11

The next step involves telling your phone that you want to use the connection to your computer to transfer files. This is usually done by pulling down from the notification area, tapping on the USB section (figure 2.12) to open up the connection options, and choosing the appropriate action (figure 2.13).

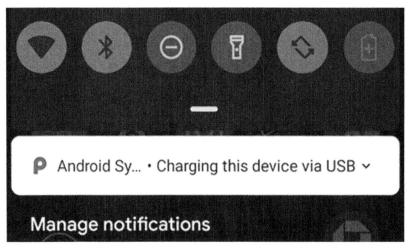

Figure 2.12

Notice in figure 2.13 that I chose the *File Transfer* option because I want to transfer files from my phone to my computer. You may see options with slightly different names such as *photo transfer,* for example. For iPhone users, you might have a popup asking if you trust this computer and you will have to say ok before being able to move on.

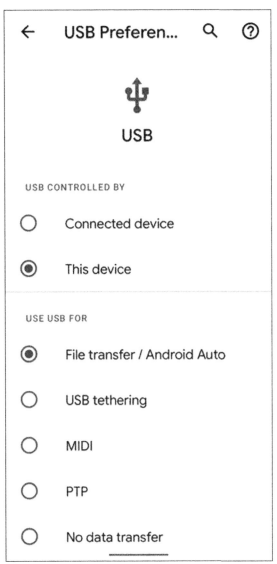

Figure 2.13

Then on my computer, I should see my phone appear. Then I can double click on its internal storage to see the files and folders contained on my phone.

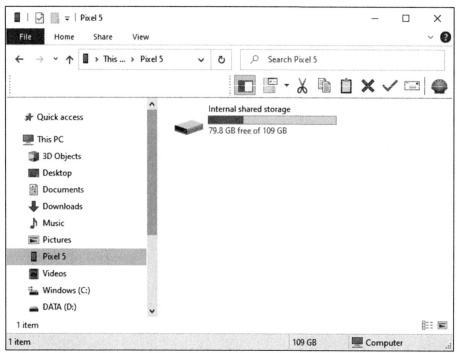

Figure 2.14

The folder I want to look for is named DCIM, and when I find that, I want to double click it to open it up.

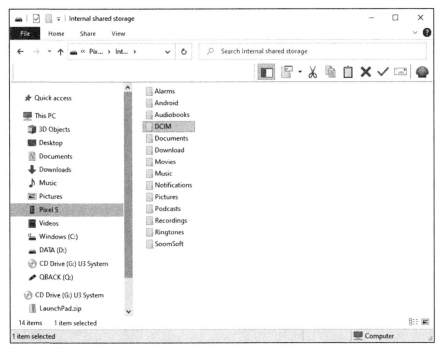

Figure 2.15

Within that folder, you may see your pictures and videos, or you might have another folder called *Camera* that you will need to open up. Once you are here, you can drag and drop the videos (or photos) from your phone to your computer and then delete them off your phone after you confirm that they have been copied over. You can delete them using the phone, or you can delete them right from this DCIM folder that you opened on your computer.

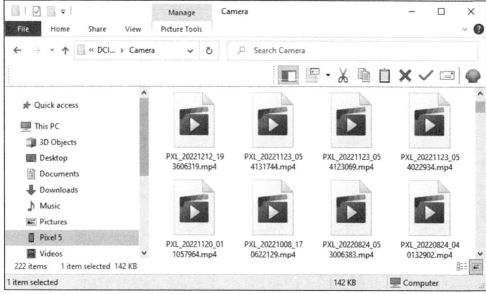

Figure 2.16

This process should be very similar for an iPhone as well as a digital camera, video camera or memory card reader.

Adding Videos to Your Timeline

Once you have your videos on your computer and have imported into Clipchamp, it's time to get them on your timeline so you can start editing them. The timeline is your work area where you will do things such as crop your video, add transitions and effects and rearrange your clips as needed.

When you start a new project, your timeline will be blank, and you will need to drag a video from your media section into the timeline. To do so, simply select the video clip you want to use and drag and drop it into the timeline at the bottom of the Clipchamp program window. Figure 2.17 shows my timeline after dragging my first video into it.

Figure 2.17

As you can see, there is a lot going on here and once you add a clip to your timeline you will have many things you can do to it. You can also see that there is a preview window above the timeline that shows your video as you edit it so you can see your results. If you need a bigger preview window or want to have your timeline more stretched out, you can hide the panels on the left and right sides of the screen by clicking the arrows on the tab for each one. Figure 2.18 shows the results.

Figure 2.18

Figure 2.19 shows a close view of the timeline where you can see the various actions you can take on your clip such as cutting, copying and deleting it. You can also add text and additional audio from here.

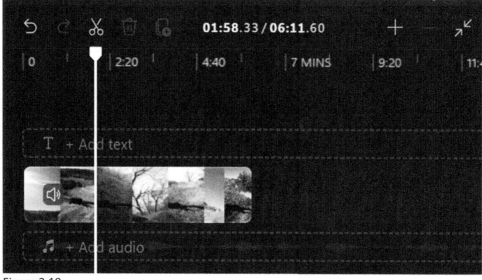

Figure 2.19

I will be going over all of these options and buttons in the next chapter when we start the editing process.

Chapter 3 – Editing Your Videos

Now that we have our videos taken and loaded into Clipchamp, it's time to start editing them so we can turn our raw footage into an Oscar winning masterpiece. Well maybe just nominated for an Oscar...

When you look at the Clipchamp interface, it can be a bit overwhelming with all of the tools and buttons that you can click on to add just about anything to your video. Once you use the software for a bit of time, you will find that you might not use many of the features that it comes with and will have your own set of go to tools that you use for all of your projects. Plus you never want to overdo a video by adding too many effects, transitions and audio clips.

The Preview Window

After you import your videos into your timeline and start working on them, you will be using the preview window to see your changes and preview your movie before you export the final version. When you click on the video in the preview window, you will get some options on the left side of the screen.

Figure 3.1

Here is what each of these options will do.

- **Fill** – This will make your video fill the preview screen.

- **Crop** – If you need to crop the dimensions of a particular clip, you can drag the size of that clip to a new size right from the preview window.

- **Picture in Picture** – In order to use the picture in picture feature, you will need to drag another video clip or image to your timeline to use for either the foreground or background picture. Then you can drag a clip along the timeline to position it so both clips line up where you want them to be. If you change your mind, you can remove one of the clips from your timeline and set the smaller clip back to Fill.

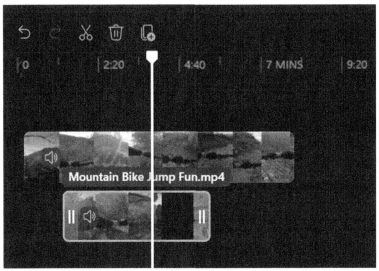

Figure 3.2

Figure 3.3

- **Rotate** – This option will rotate your video 90 degrees each time that you click the button.

- **Flip Horizontal** – This can be used to reverse your video clip.

- **Flip Vertical** – This will flip your video clip so it's upside down. Sometimes you may run across a situation where your camera recorded upside down so this is a good way to fix your footage.

At the bottom of the preview window, you will have your play button as well as a button to skip back 5 seconds and forward 5 seconds. The button at the very left will take you to the previous clip in your timeline while the button at the right will take you to the next clip in your timeline. If you only have one clip at the beginning or end of your timeline, then it will take you to the beginning or end of that clip.

Figure 3.4

At the very right bottom corner of the preview window, you will see a box shaped icon that will make your preview show in full screen mode.

The Editing Timeline

The timeline is where you will be performing most of your video editing functions and I want to take a moment to go over all the features of the timeline so you have an understanding of what they will all do.

Figure 3.5 shows my timeline with two video clips within it and when you select a clip, it will be highlighted so you can take certain actions on that clip. The vertical line that is on top of the second clip is the time marker which is what determines what is shown in the preview window. You can drag the time marker around with your mouse to position it anywhere you like so you don't have to wait for a clip to play through to get your marker in the place where you need it to be.

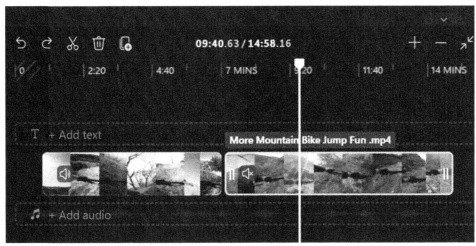

Figure 3.5

At the top of the timeline, you will see various time positions which indicate how long your video will be at that particular point. Where the time marker in figure 3.5 is located is around 9:40 (9 minutes and 40 seconds) into the total length of the video. Above these time points you will see the exact time as well as the total time. So far, my video is 14 minutes and 58 seconds long.

At the top left of the timeline, you will have various icons that perform different functions. From left to right these functions are undo, redo, split (cut), delete and duplicate. Just be sure you are on the right clip before selecting delete or duplicate. The split function will cut your clip into two sections based on the position of the timeline marker.

Figure 3.6

At the top right of the timeline, you will have options to zoom in, zoom out and make your clips take up the length of the timeline (zoom to fit). This will not affect your preview window but rather how the clips fit on the timeline.

Figure 3.7

You will also notice that there are *add text* and *add audio* choices above and below the timeline. This is just another way to get to the same features that are on the toolbar at the left of the screen which I will be going over later in this chapter.

As you start adding items such as graphics or additional audio to your video, you will start to see that your timeline will begin to have more layers and you may find that you need to drag a layer above another layer to make it display correctly. For example, if you add some text and find that it's being covered up by a graphic, you might need to rearrange your text layer so it's on top of the graphic layer.

Trimming and Splitting Video Clips

There is a very good chance that you will not want to use all the footage from your video clips for your final movie and will need to crop out some of it so it can be removed. Or you may want to take part of your footage and move it to a different part of the timeline such as after a different clip.

Fortunately, this is very easy to do using the Split tool which is the icon that looks like a pair of scissors above the timeline. To use the Split tool, you will need to place the timeline marker where you want to cut the clip and then click on the Split tool to have your clip separated into two individual clips.

Before

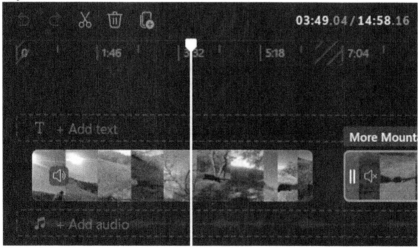

Figure 3.8

After

Figure 3.9

Now I can rearrange my clip sections as needed or even delete one of it was just some extra footage that I wanted to crop out of my video. Figure 3.10 shows how I moved one part of my split clip to the end of a completely different clip.

Figure 3.10

Video Transitions and Fading

Once you have multiple clips on your timeline you may want to add a transition or fade effect to a clip so one doesn't just end and the other simply begins. These transitions are used to "blend" clips together such as the first one fading out and the next one fading in or maybe even one clip spinning into the next.

To use a transition, you will need to place them between two clips on your timeline. If you want to add a transition to the end of your final clip, then you would need to use a fade. There are two main things you need to be aware of when using transitions. One is that there can't be any blank or empty space between your clips so you will need to make sure they are continuous or touching. The other is that if you simply snip a clip and then join the two parts together, you might not be able to add a transition because Clipchamp still sees it as one continuous piece of footage.

There are a couple of ways to add a transition to your timeline. One way is to go to the Transitions panel by clicking on the *Transitions* button within the left hand toolbar. Then you will be able to see the available transitions and can then drag the one you want between the clips where you would like it to be placed.

Figure 3.11

The method I like to use is to click in between the clips where you want the transition to be placed and then click on the *Add transition* button. Then you will see the transition choices open up on the right side of the screen where you can then select the one you would like to use. One thing to be aware of is that if you are zoomed out too far on your timeline, you may not be able to get the Add transition button to appear.

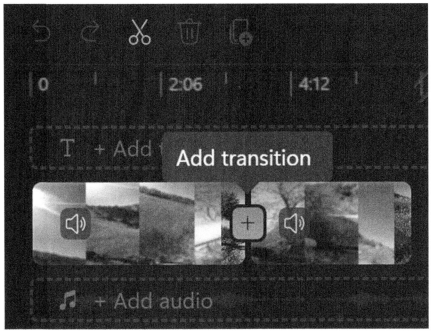

Figure 3.12

When using this method you will see your transition options on the right side of the screen but this time you will be able to adjust the duration regarding how long they appear between your clips as seen in figure 3.13. You can also choose a different transition from here if needed.

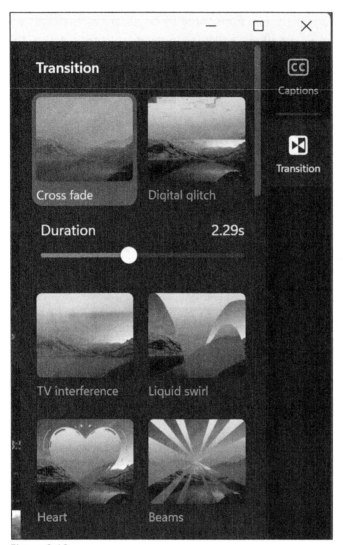

Figure 3.13

As you increase the duration, you will notice a green highlight on the end of the first clip and the beginning of the second clip indicating how much of the clips the transition applies to. You can also make duration adjustments to existing transitions by clicking on them to select them. If you want to remove a transition, simply right click on it and choose *Delete*.

You can also use the fade option to have the ending of one clip fade out or the beginning of another clip fade in. To do so, select the clip you wish to apply the fade to and then click the *Fade* button at the top right of the window. Then you will be able to select your fade duration up to two seconds in length.

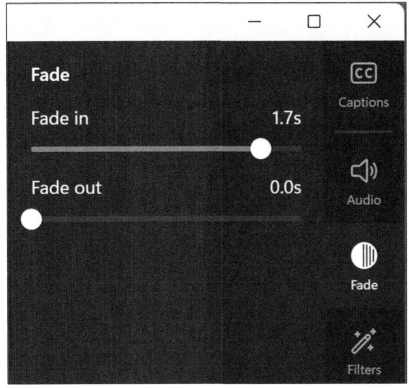

Figure 3.14

Adding Music and Other Audio

Clipchamp comes with a selection of music and sound effects that you can use with your video. Some of it is free to use and others are only available to those who have the paid subscription plan. Regardless, you will be shown which audio clips you can use for free, and which are the premium types.

If you click on the *Music & SFX section*, you will be shown various music and sound effects audio that you can preview by pressing the play button. They are broken down into categories and you can click on the *See more* button to view additional clips in that category.

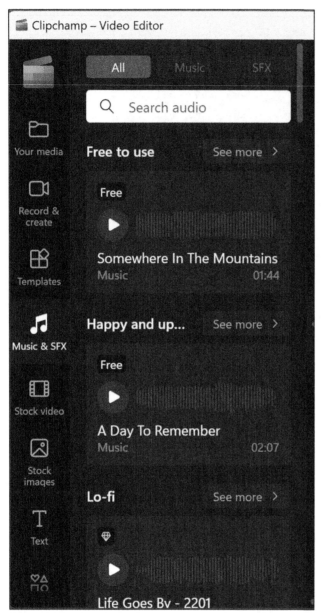

Figure 3.15

You will know when an audio clip is for premium users because it will have a gold diamond icon above the play button as shown in figure 3.16. You will be able to preview the clip but won't be able to use it in your video if you don't have a premium membership.

Figure 3.16

Once you find an audio clip you like, simply click on the Add to timeline + button next to the clip and it will be placed on your timeline.

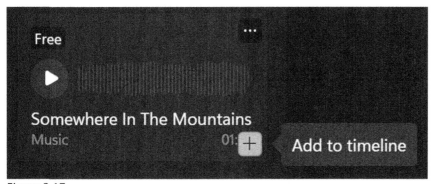

Figure 3.17

You will then most likely need to position the clip on your timeline under your existing video clip, so the music or sound effect matches up with your video. These clips will not replace the audio in your existing video but rather play along with it.

Figure 3.18 shows a music clip that I added to my video but as you can see, the music clip is not long enough to play for the length of the video. When this happens you can either shorten your video clip by cropping out some footage or adding another music clip or even repeating the same clip over again. You can do so by right clicking on a clip and choosing the *duplicate* or *copy* option.

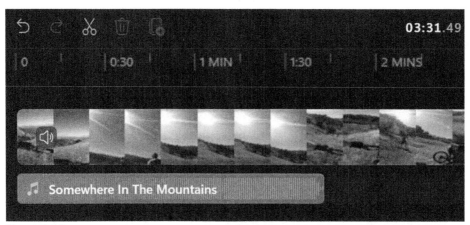

Figure 3.18

If you want to add your own audio file such as an MP3 music file or maybe a voice recording you have made, you can do so from the Your media section and import it like you would a video file. You can also go to the Record & create section and record something on the spot.

Adjusting Audio Volume & Detaching Audio
Getting your volume levels correct is an important part of making a presentable video. If you have multiple clips with different volume levels, then you don't want your viewers to have to turn their volume up and down to match the levels you have in your video. You want to try and have a constant volume level throughout all of your clips unless of course you really want to emphasize something with a burst of volume.

If you have added additional audio such as music or sound effects, then you want to make sure that they do not drown out the audio that was recorded with your video or vice versa. This is why it's important to preview your entire video before exporting the final version.

To adjust the volume level for a clip, you can click on it to select it and then click on the *Audio* button at the top right of the editor. You will then have a volume slider that you can drag from 0 to 100%. Then you should preview your change to make sure it's at the right level.

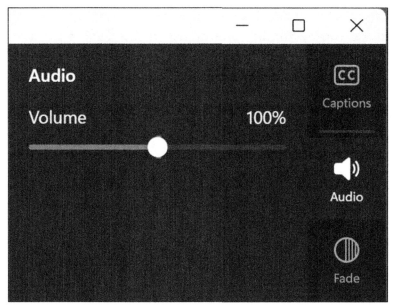

Figure 3.19

One thing you might want to do before splitting up your clips into multiple smaller clips is adjust the volume for the entire clip, so you don't need to go back and fix it for each of your separate clips.

When you click on a clip that contains video footage with audio and then click the Audio button, you will see that you have a button labeled *Detach audio* (figure 3.20). This is used to separate the video from the audio on a clip that has both attributes. You can do this if you want to use the audio portion somewhere else or just remove it from the clip altogether.

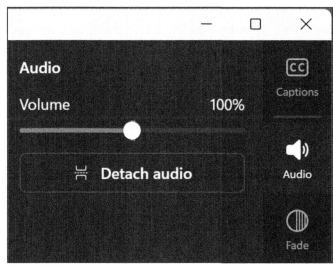

Figure 3.20

Figure 3.21 shows a clip titled Mountain Bike Jump Fun that was cut using the Split tool. Then I selected the clip on the left and detached the audio from it and Clipchamp then placed it on its own line on the timeline with a matching name but put (Audio) in front of it to indicate it is audio only and not video.

Figure 3.21

You might notice that Clipchamp will automatically download the detached audio to your computer in case you want a copy of the standalone audio file.

Inserting Text

Adding text to your video is a fun way to point out various events or locations that you might not have mentioned while filming the video. The process for inserting text is very simple and you have quite a few text styles to choose from if you want to spice things up a bit rather than just use plain text.

Figure 3.22

Once you choose your text style, it will automatically be placed on your timeline where you can then click on it to edit the text itself, its position in your video and change how long it stays on the screen.

Figure 3.23 shows that I have chosen some text with four stars and once I click on the text block in the timeline, I can then change the text and the font at the upper right of the editor. I can then drag the text box in the preview screen to the right position and resize it if needed. To adjust where the text shows and for how long, I can move the text block in the timeline and also shrink or enlarge it to determine how long it stays on the screen.

Figure 3.23

Using Stock Images and Videos

Stock images and stock videos are terms used for photos and videos created by others that are meant to be used by people like us for our videos and artwork etc. There are free photos and videos that anyone can use and then there are the "premium" types that will cost you money if you wish to use them in one of your projects.

Clipchamp comes with both free and premium versions, and you can browse through both and will be shown which ones are free and which are not. When you click on Stock videos on the toolbar at the left side of the editor, you will be shown samples of images from various categories. I don't find these too useful for my videos, but you may find some that you like for yours.

Figure 3.24 shows some of the categories, and if I click on the arrow in one of those categories such as Video frames, I will be shown more images related to that category (figure 3.25).

Figure 3.24

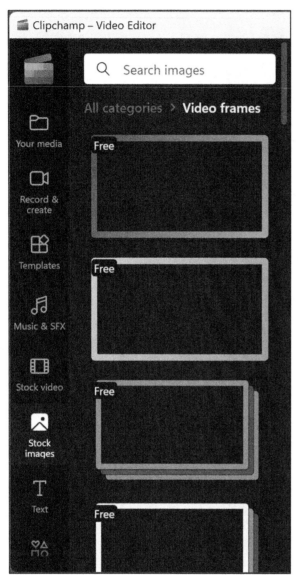

Figure 3.25

I will now choose a border and have it added to my video. Figure 3.26 shows how it works the same way that adding text works and you can move it around and specify how long it will stay in your video. I will also have the option to have the image fade in and fade out as it's displayed within the video.

Figure 3.26

Figure 3.27 shows some of the options for the stock videos. These work differently than images because most of them are videos that work like the clips you added from your own camera. Some of them will play alongside or within your existing videos while others are meant to be used in between your clips or even as a picture in picture option.

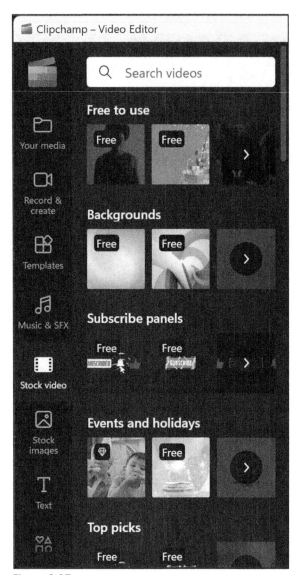

Figure 3.27

Figure 3.28 shows a subscribe video inserted within an existing video clip that also has its own sound with it. You obviously can't see the video animation will have to take my word for it that it's an actual video clip within an existing clip.

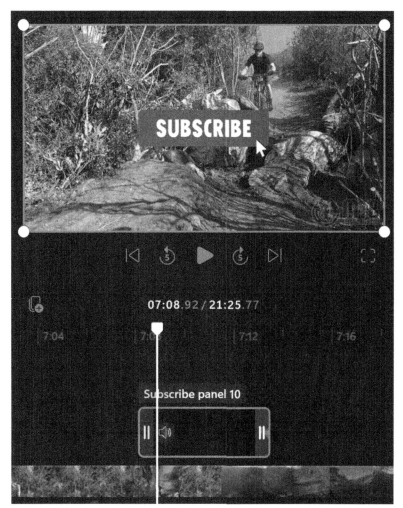

Figure 3.28

Adding Graphics

Clipchamp comes with a selection of built in graphics that you can add to your video. These graphics can be static images, or they may have an animation such as an animated GIF file. You add them to your project just like you would with an image that I just discussed in the section on stock images.

Figure 3.29

Figure 3.30 shows how I added a speech bubble and then also added a text layer to go inside the speech bubble. Once you have your graphic in place, you can then determine where it is displayed in your video and for how long by manipulating it on the timeline.

Figure 3.30

You can also add your own graphics just like you would any other media type such as a video or audio file.

Changing the Video Speed

One thing you may want to do when editing your video is either speed up or slow down the speed of a particular clip. Let's say you want to make a slow motion clip of your child sliding into home plate or maybe speed up a section of your video that might be a little repetitive or taking too long to finish. Fortunately, this is a very easy thing to do in the Clipchamp editor.

The key thing to remember when changing the speed of your video is that it will apply to the entire clip. So if you only want a certain section of a clip sped up or slowed down, you will need to use the Split tool to separate out that part of the clip. Then you can use the Speed option to adjust how fast or slow that part of the clip is by clicking on the Speed icon on the right side of the editor.

Figure 3.31 shows my cropped clip and over to the right, you can see that the speed is set to 1x which is the original speed. As you can see, you have the option to lower the speed as low as .1x the original and up to 16x the original. You can also use increments such as .5 and 2.5 for example by using the slider or by typing the exact number in the box.

Figure 3.31

Figure 3.32 shows what happens when I set the speed of that clip to 2x the original speed. As you can see, the clip itself shrinks to accommodate the faster speed and I will then need to delete the blank area in between my sped up clip and the next clip, otherwise I will have a black screen during that part of the video. If I were to slow down the video, the selected clip would become larger and push all the clips to the right of it more to the right of the timeline.

Figure 3.32

Adding Filters

Filters are a great way to add some artistic flair to your footage or to make a clip stand out amongst the others in your video. Clipchamp has many built in filters that you can apply to your video but when doing so, you will need to use the Split tool to separate the section of the clip you want to have it applied to, otherwise it will be applied to the entire clip.

Figure 3.33 shows that I have applied an Old Western filter to a specific clip. When you apply a filter, your preview window will show how that filter will look on your video and you can then adjust its intensity to make it stronger as needed.

Figure 3.33

Adjusting Colors

Many times you will find that your camera did not do the best job of capturing your footage the way you intended it to do. Your video might come out too light, too dark or maybe lacking in color. Fortunately, Clipchamp has some fairly decent color adjustments that you can apply to your video clips.

Once you select the clip you want to adjust, simply click on the *Adjust colors* icon on the right side of the editor interface. You will then be presented with options to adjust the exposure, saturation, temperature and contrast by using the sliders underneath each option. You will be shown how these changes will be applied to your video as you make the adjustments.

Figure 3.34

The *Blend mode* and *Opacity* slider are used to make adjustments when you have two videos overlayed on top of each other so if you try and use these on a single video clip, it will not change anything.

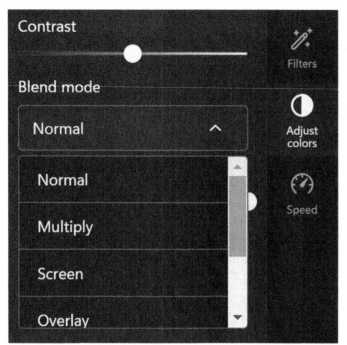

Figure 3.35

Chapter 4 – Exporting Your Video

Once you have your video and all of its effects, sounds and transitions in place, it's finally time to export your work so you can share it with friends, family or anyone else willing to watch it!

Depending on how much editing you have done and how many additions you have placed on your timeline, your timeline itself may look a little "busy." This is perfectly fine if that is the theme you are going for. Just remember that sometimes less is more when it comes to adding effects etc. to your videos.

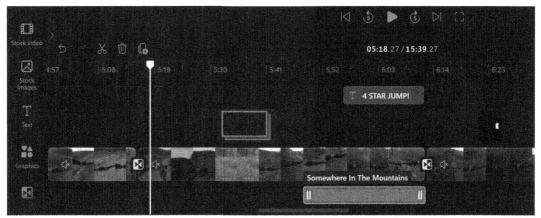

Figure 4.1

Before you actually export your video, there are a few things you might want to check over or adjust so your final copy looks the way you intended it to look.

Changing the Video Aspect Ratio
By default, Clipchamp will adjust the video aspect ratio to match your footage. For my project, the aspect ratio is 16:9 which is the typical widescreen format you see on computer monitors and TVs.

If you shot your video on your phone and were holding it vertically, your aspect ratio might be 9:16 or something similar. Figure 4.2 shows the common aspect ratio settings you can use in your project.

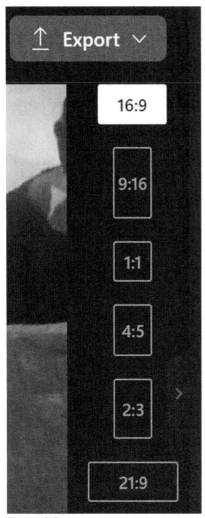

Figure 4.2

If you decide to change this setting, you need to be aware that you will most likely end up with some black bars on the top and bottom or left and right side of your video since Clipchamp will try and fit your video into this new aspect ratio.

Figure 4.3 shows what happens when I choose the 21:9 setting, and you can see it ends up putting black bars on the left and right side of the video to fill the extra space needed by the larger setting.

Figure 4.3

Figure 4.4 shows what happens if I switch to a vertical style 2:3 setting. As you can see, I get some large black bars above and below my video and the viewable space is much smaller to make it fit in the reduced width of this particular aspect ratio.

Figure 4.4

Export Options

When it comes to exporting your video to a file, you do not have too many options to choose from. This should be ok for most home users, but if you are trying to make professional high quality videos, you might find the options a little lacking.

One thing you most likely will see when you first click on the Export button at the top right of the editor window is a message about having extra gaps in your timeline. It gives you this warning because having a gap in your main footage will leave a blank or black screen for the duration of the gap size.

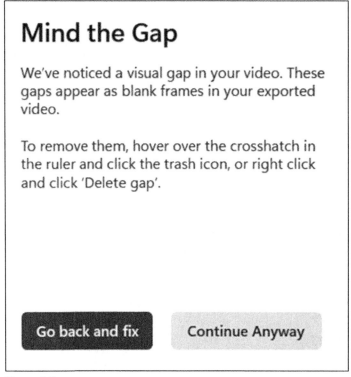

Mind the Gap

We've noticed a visual gap in your video. These gaps appear as blank frames in your exported video.

To remove them, hover over the crosshatch in the ruler and click the trash icon, or right click and click 'Delete gap'.

Go back and fix   Continue Anyway

Figure 4.5

Figure 4.6 shows a gap between two video clips and if you place the mouse between the gap, you will be shown a trash can icon that you can click on to close the gap and make the two clips continuous. You can also drag one clip to the other to manually close the gap or shrink the gap if you do want some blank footage between the clips.

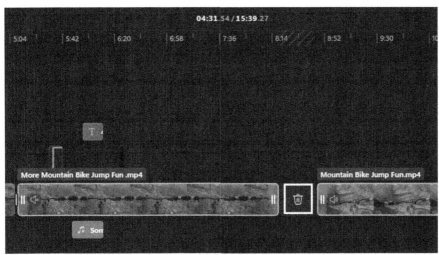

Figure 4.6

Even after you close the gap between your clips, you might still get the same message when exporting your video if you have gaps between text, graphics or audio effects as seen in figure 4.7.

Figure 4.7

In this case, you most likely don't want to delete the gap because it will move your effect out of the position you originally placed it so you can simply click the *Continue Anyway* button on the message shown in figure 4.5.

Next, you will be presented with a few options for the video quality for your exported project. As you can see in figure 4.8, your export options are limited.

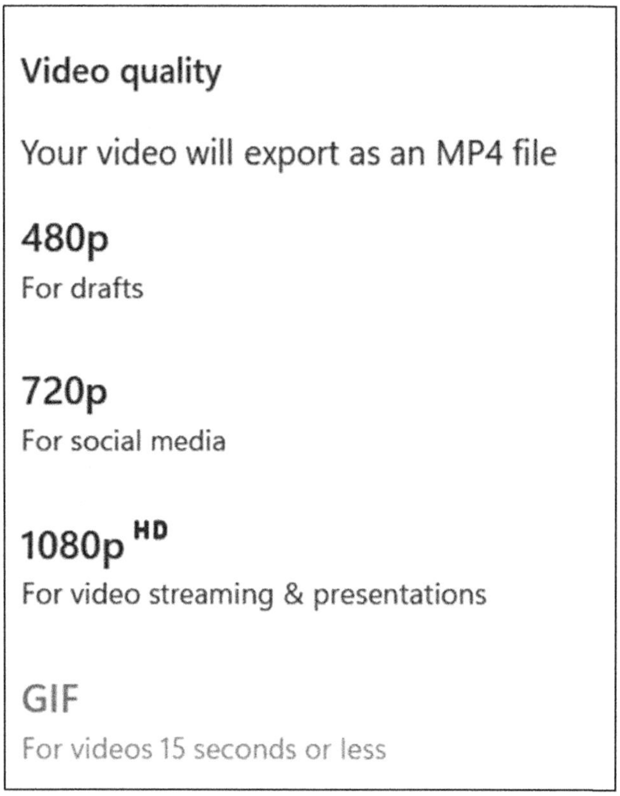

Video quality

Your video will export as an MP4 file

480p
For drafts

720p
For social media

1080p **HD**
For video streaming & presentations

GIF
For videos 15 seconds or less

Figure 4.8

For the most part, you will want to use the HD 1080p setting even if you plan to use the video online for sites such as YouTube or Facebook. Unfortunately, there is no 4k setting so if your original footage was shot in 4k, it will be downgraded and most likely not look as sharp as the original video.

Once you choose your video quality setting, the export process will begin automatically, and you will be shown a preview screen of the export as it's happening. If your movie is on the longer side, be prepared to wait a while for the export is completed. And if your computer hardware is not the fastest, it might take even longer.

Figure 4.9

On the export screen, you will see a button that says *Create video link*. This can be used to upload your video to the Clipchamp website so you can share it via a link that can be emailed out to whomever you want to be able to watch your video. You will also have some additional buttons such as emailing the link or using Facebook Messenger or WhatsApp to share the link.

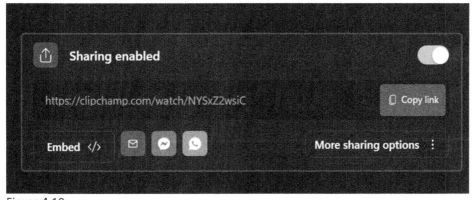

Figure 4.10

Clicking on *More sharing options* will give you some additional selections such create a link to embed your video on a website as well as other sharing options such as creating a post on your Facebook or Reddit account.

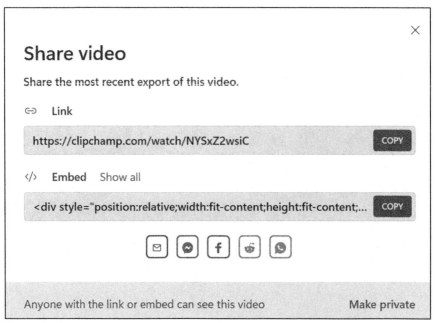

Figure 4.11

Figure 4.12 shows some additional ways to save or share your video. If you have a Google Drive or Dropbox account for example, you can connect it to your Clipchamp account by logging in to the corresponding account and giving Clipchamp access to copy your video to your account. Just keep in mind that these exported videos can be large in size and if you are limited on the amount of space you have in your account, you might end up using it all up.

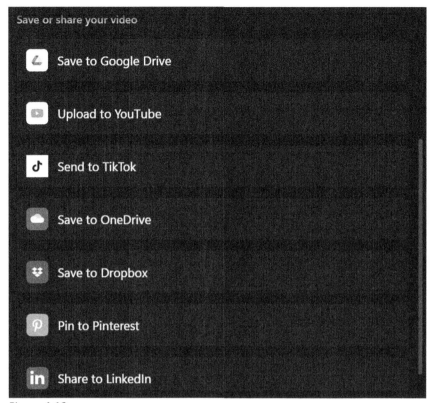

Figure 4.12

Now that my video export is complete, I will have a button that says *Save to your computer*.

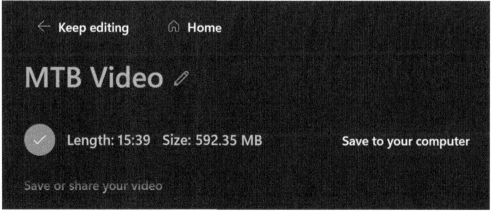

Figure 4.13

Even if I don't click that button, Clipchamp will automatically save my exported video to my Downloads folder, and I will be shown a box telling me so. If you don't see this box, you can simply go to your Downloads folder (Windows PCs) to see your video file (figure 4.15).

Figure 4.14

As you can see from figure 4.15, my video is about 578 MB in size.

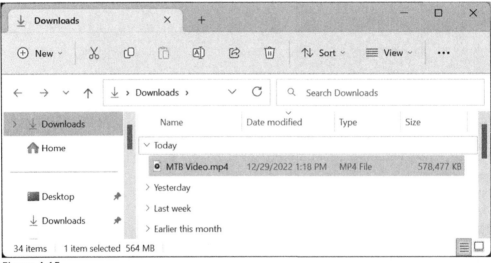

Figure 4.15

If I right click on my video file and choose *Properties*, I can then go to the *Details* tab to see the video length (15:39) and its resolution which is 1920x1080. I can also see that is has been exported at 30 fps (frames per second).

Figure 4.16

Now I can do things such as burn it to a DVD or upload it to YouTube or another video sharing website. I can also watch it on my computer by double clicking on the file itself.

Uploading Your Video to YouTube

As you saw earlier in this chapter, you have the option to share your video with various social media sites such as Facebook and TikTok etc. One of the more popular video sharing sites is YouTube of course so now I would like to go over the process to share your video from Clipchamp directly to your YouTube account. If you are a regular YouTube user, you know that you can also upload your exported video file to your channel as another way to share your work.

The first time you upload your video to YouTube, you will need to connect your YouTube account to Clipchamp so it will have access to upload your video file.

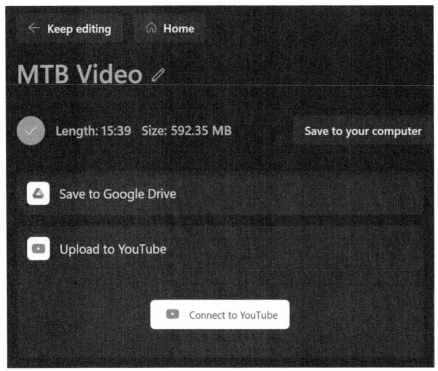

Figure 4.17

If you have more than one Google\YouTube account, you will need to select the one you want to use for the video upload.

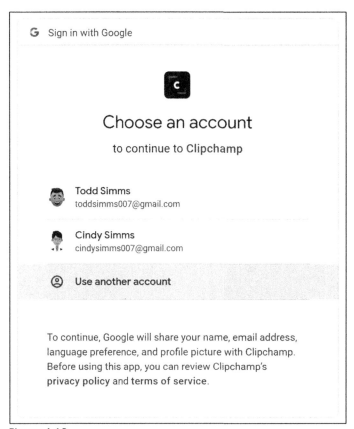

Figure 4.18

Next, you will be told what permissions Clipchamp needs in order to upload your video to your YouTube channel, and you must click the *Allow* button to continue.

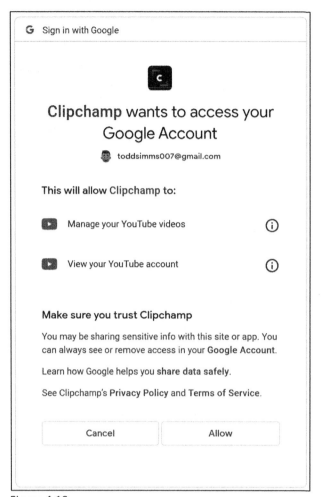

Figure 4.19

Then you may get a popup asking to open Clipchamp in order to start the upload process. If you already have Clipchamp open, you can still click on the *Open Clipchamp* button. If you plan to upload to YouTube on a regular basis, you can select the checkbox that says *Always allow app.clipchamp.com to open links of this type in the associated app.*

Open Clipchamp – Video Editor?

https://app.clipchamp.com wants to open this application.

☐ Always allow app.clipchamp.com to open links of this type in the associated app

Open Clipchamp – Video Editor   Cancel

Figure 4.20

Next, you will be able to fill in information about your video that will be used when it's posted to your YouTube account. You can enter the title and description as well as decide if you want the video public or private and you can also set a category if desired. The *keywords* section is used to help others find your video when searching for matching keywords. Unless your video is specifically made for kids, you should check the radio button that says *No, it's not made for kids*.

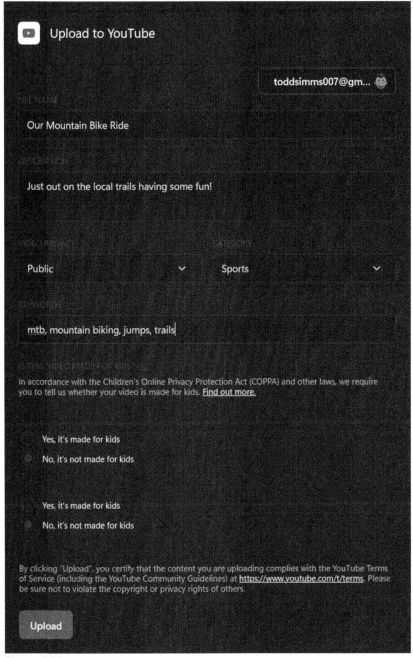

Figure 4.21

Once everything looks good, simply click on the *Upload* button to begin the upload process. You will then be told that the upload will begin after the export process is completed.

If you close the Clipchamp editor after exporting your video the first time, it will want to export it again before uploading it to YouTube so try and do all of your sharing before shutting Clipchamp down.

When the upload is complete, you will be shown a link to the video on YouTube that you can copy and send out to others. You can also log into your YouTube account and see your video posted there as well.

Figure 4.22

Chapter 5 – Additional Features

As you have seen so far, importing, editing and exporting videos is a fairly simple process in Clipchamp and compared to more advanced video editing software such as Adobe Premiere, it's very easy to use.

There are some additional features that you might want to check out as well as some settings you can adjust to make Clipchamp work a little better for you. In this chapter, I will be going over these settings and additional features.

Brand Kits

If you are creating videos for something such as a product or service, you might want to check out the brand kit feature. This is only available for the paid subscription accounts and not the free accounts. If you click on Brand Kit from the left side of the editor, you will see a screen similar to figure 5.1 but you will also see that there is a gold diamond on the *Build your brand kit* button indicating that it is a premium feature.

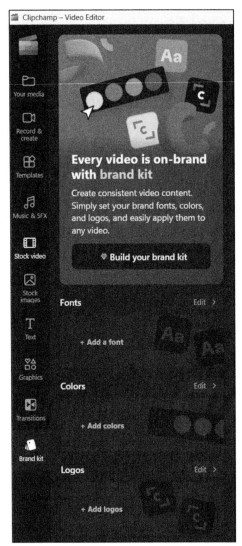

Figure 5.1

Brand kits are used to store your personal fonts, colors and logos that correspond with your brand. That way, you have a uniform set of design tools that you can apply to all of your videos to give them a consistent overall look. This helps keep your "brand" recognizable and gives your videos a more professional overall appearance.

Once you have your fonts, colors and logos uploaded, you can then access them during the video editing process as needed. You can also add and remove brand kit items if your overall theme needs to be changed.

Brand kits are part of the Essentials subscription which will cost you $11.99 per month or $119.99 for a year.

Templates

If you prefer not to start with a blank canvas for your video, you can use one of the many built in templates that come included with Clipchamp. These templates consist of preconfigured graphics, text, music and effects that you can customize with your own content.

To add a template simply click on the *Templates* icon from the left hand toolbar and you will be presented with several categories as shown in figure 5.2. There is also a search box at the top of the list that you can use to find specific template themes.

Figure 5.2

For my example, I will select the YouTube category and will then be shown various templates that are related to YouTube videos.

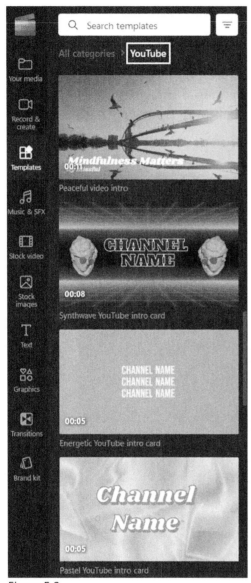

Figure 5.3

I will then choose the template called *Synthwave YouTube intro card*. I will then be prompted to either add this template to my timeline or create a new project using this template. I will choose the first option.

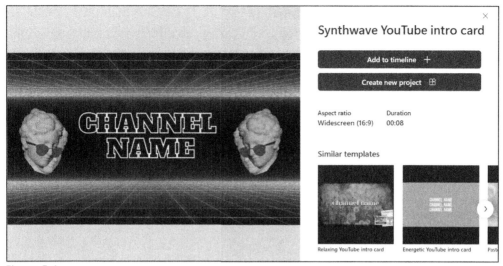

Figure 5.4

As you can see in figure 5.5, the template has been placed on the timeline and it includes several components such as music, graphics, text and animations. I can then customize these components by moving them around, stretching them out and changing the text etc. I can also add my own elements to the timeline if I want to customize things even more.

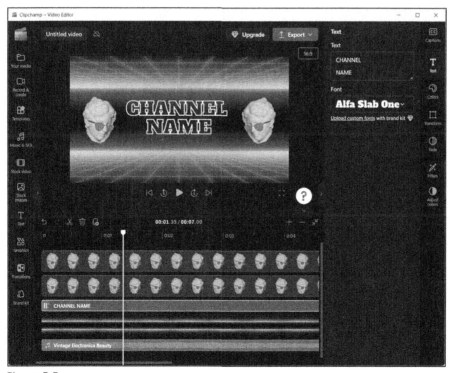

Figure 5.5

Creating Folders & Organizing Videos

If you plan on creating multiple videos on a variety of different subjects or are just simply the type of person who likes to keep things in order, then you can create folders to keep your video projects organized.

By default, Clipchamp will store all of your projects in the main area of the Home page. But if you look at the upper left corner while on the Home page, you will see an option to create a new folder.

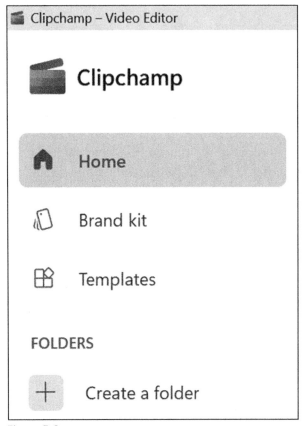

Figure 5.6

Once you click on *Create a folder*, you will be prompted to enter a name for this new folder. I will call mine MTB videos and also make another folder for future dog videos.

New folder

Enter folder name

MTB Videos

Create folder   Cancel

Figure 5.7

Figure 5.8 shows my Home page with my two new folders.

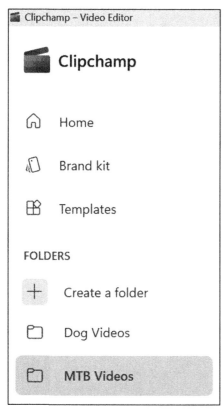

Figure 5.8

To move an existing project into a folder, simply click on the ellipsis (...) at the upper right corner of the video and choose the *Move* option.

Figure 5.9

Then you will need to choose one of your folders to move the project into and click the *Move here* button. Then you will be able to find your project under that folder on the Home page.

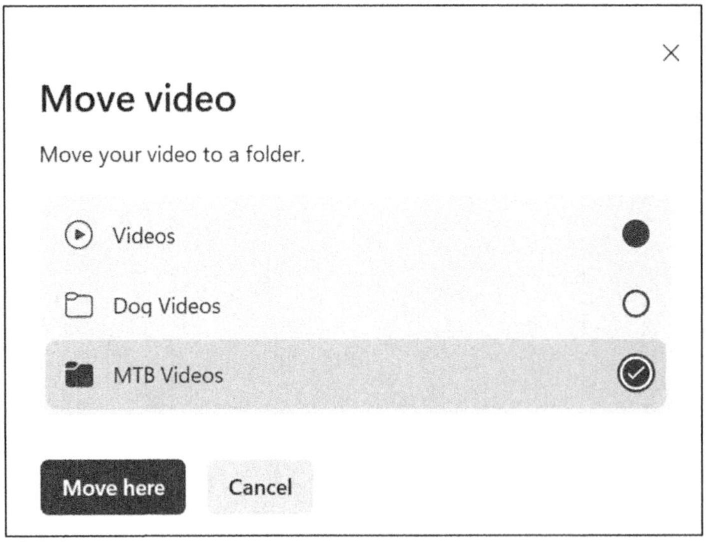

Figure 5.10

Making Photos Fill the Screen

When you add your own pictures to your video, there is a good chance they will not match the size of your video. For example, a 1080p video has dimensions of

1920 x 1080 pixels. A high quality cellphone picture might have 4032 x 2268 for its dimensions, or an older picture might use 720 x 480.

So if your picture does not match the video size you are using then it will either be too big for the screen or not fill up the screen and leave black bars on the sides or the top and bottom.

Figure 5.11 shows a picture that was placed into my video that is smaller than the video dimensions of the video itself. As you can see, there is some extra space on the left and right of the picture that will be filled with black bars, and it will not take up the entire screen when the video gets to this picture.

Fortunately, you have a couple of options to fix this problem depending on if your picture is too large or too small for your video.

Figure 5.11

If the picture is too small, you can use the fill option to force it to fill the screen. Just be aware that when Clipchamp makes your image fit the screen that it will crop out the edges to make it fit as shown in figure 5.12. Even after the picture is resized to fit, you can drag it around the preview window to adjust which part of the picture will be shown in the video.

Figure 5.12

If your image is too big for the screen, you can still use the fill option to have it shrunk down or you can use the crop option to crop out the section of the photo you would like to use. Regardless of its size, Clipchamp will place it in the preview window and try and make it fit.

Figure 5.13 shows a picture that is larger than my video size and doesn't fit the screen. This time I will use the crop option to crop out just the part of the picture I want to use. You can also accomplish this by dragging and stretching or shrinking the picture manually using the circles that appear in the corners when it's selected.

Figure 5.13

Once I crop the image to my liking, I can click on the checkmark icon to apply my changes or the undo arrow to reverse the cropping process.

Figure 5.14

I can then drag the image to the exact position I want in the preview window and that is how it will look when it plays in my video.

Figure 5.15

Closed Captions

If your video is going to be viewed by those with hearing impairments or maybe in an environment where you can't have the sound turned up too loud, you can use the closed caption feature to have the dialog of your video displayed on the screen as it's played.

Before using this feature, keep in mind that it might not be perfect and may not translate all of your speech 100% correctly. Plus if you have a lot of background noise or more than one person speaking, then that might make it even harder for Clipchamp to perform the translation.

To apply the captions to your video, click on the *Captions* button at the top right of the screen and then click on the *Turn on auto-captions* button.

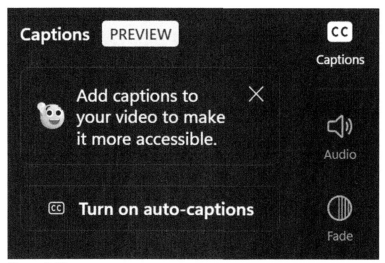

Figure 5.16

Next, you will be able to choose your language and have the option to filter out profanity if needed. Once you have everything set, click on the *Turn on auto-captions* button once again.

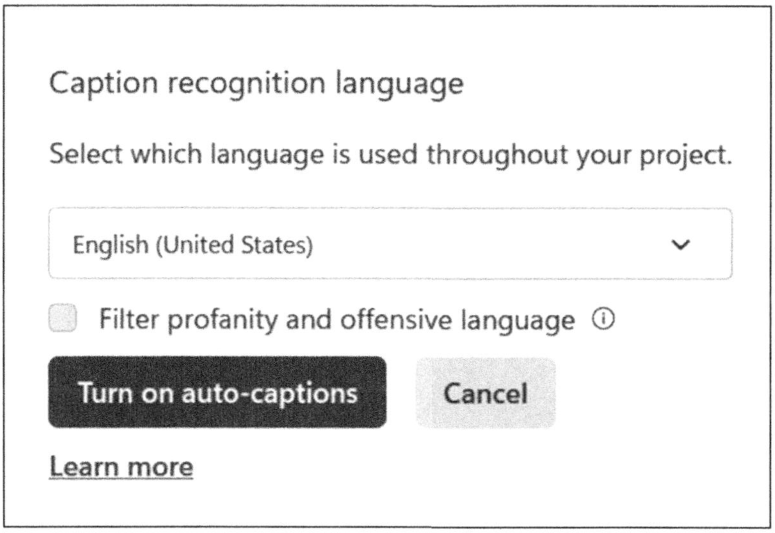

Caption recognition language

Select which language is used throughout your project.

English (United States)

Filter profanity and offensive language ⓘ

Turn on auto-captions   Cancel

Learn more

Figure 5.17

Clipchamp will then go through your video and process all the voice audio it hears and start converting it to on screen text.

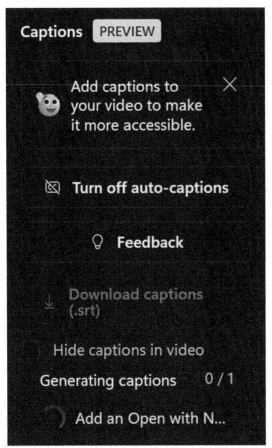

Figure 5.18

You will then be able to see your text off to the side of the video preview screen along with time stamps of when the specific text occurred.

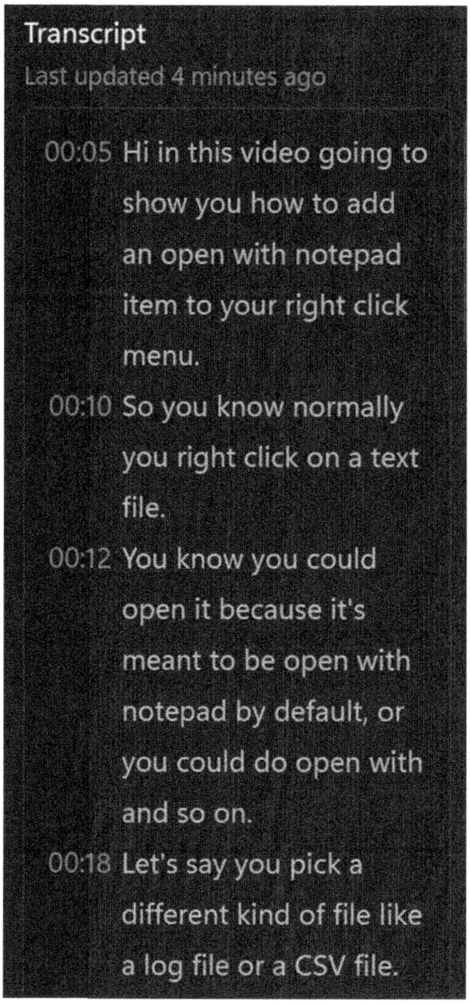

Figure 5.19

You will also be able to see your captions in the preview window in real time as you play your video.

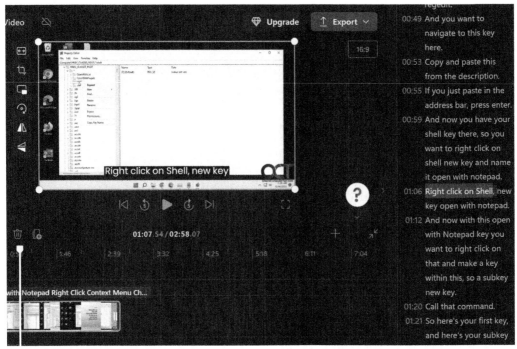

Figure 5.20

Backing Up and Importing Your Project

As you probably know, backing up the data on your computer is a critical task that everyone should be performing on a regular basis. And if you want to ensure that your Clipchamp projects are safe, then you might want to think about backing them up as well.

Since Clipchamp is a Windows app, it's not quite the same as a Windows program such as Adobe Premiere for example which lets you save your project in a folder of your choosing. Clipchamp automatically saves your work every five seconds but doesn't allow you to specify where to save it to. And if you are using the web based version, you have even less control.

So when it comes to backing up your projects, you have two options. If you have the subscription plan, you can have your project and its associated files backed up to the cloud and then if you get a new computer, all you need to do is log in with the same account and all of your videos and pictures etc. will be there waiting for you.

While in your project, you can click on the cloud icon next to the project name to enable the automatic backup. If you don't have a subscription, you will see a message similar to what is shown in figure 5.21.

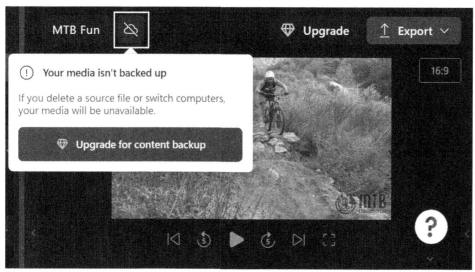

Figure 5.21

If you plan to use Clipchamp a lot or for important videos, you can consider the paid subscription plan to be able to use this backup option.

If you would rather not pay for this feature, you can backup your videos and photos yourself like you would any other files on your computer. Then if you have to switch computers or had some unfortunate data loss, you can then restore your files from your backup and log into Clipchamp again.

The one thing you will need to worry about is if you restore your files to a different location on your computer than where they were before or if you change their name because Clipchamp will not be able to load them into your project if it can't find them.

Figure 5.22 shows what happens when I log into Clipchamp on a different computer and try to open the same video project I had open on the other computer. As you can see, Clipchamp can't find my videos and photos because they are not on this computer but rather on the other computer where I originally started my project.

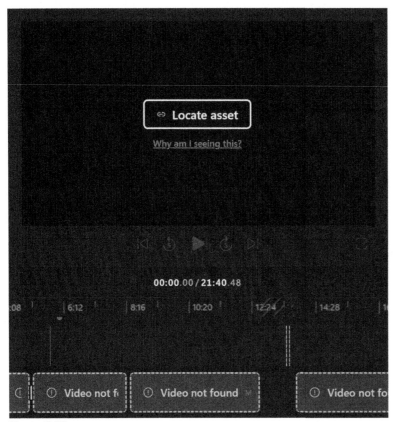

Figure 5.22

When I click on one of the video clips, I am shown a window with a list of the missing files. I can then click on *Locate folder* to browse my computer for the location of the media that Clipchamp is looking for, assuming I have a copy on this other computer.

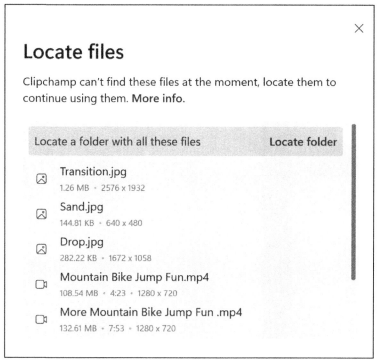

Figure 5.23

So if you do need to open your project on a new or different computer, you can copy your media files over and place them all in a folder and then tell Clipchamp where they are located, and you should be able to open your project and continue where you left off.

Keyboard Shortcuts

Keyboard shortcuts are nothing new and most Windows and Mac programs will either have their own specific keyboard shortcuts or allow you to use the shortcuts that come with the operating system. Some common Windows examples would include Ctrl-C for copy and Ctrl-V for paste.

Clipchamp will let you use most of the operating system keyboard shortcuts but also includes its own shortcuts to help you work more efficiently when working on your projects. For example, you can use Alt-E to go to the export menu or Ctrl-0 to make your media files fit the timeline.

To see the available keyboard shortcuts, you can click on the three vertical lines at the upper left corner of the editor window (also known as the hamburger menu) and then click on *Keyboard shortcuts*.

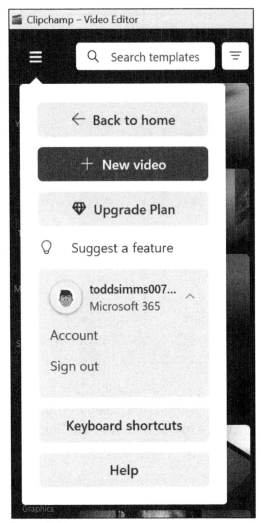

Figure 5.24

You will then be shown a list of all of the available shortcuts (figure 5.25) and will also notice how they included universal shortcuts such as Ctrl-C and Ctrl-V which I had just mentioned. You can scroll down the list to see the entire listing of keyboard shortcuts so you can become familiar with them.

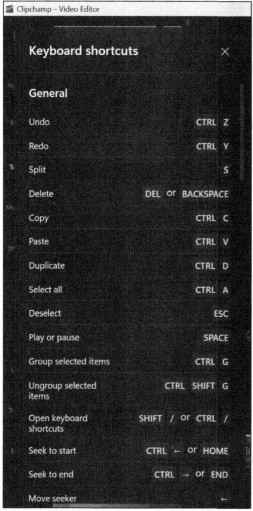

Figure 5.25

Getting Help

Even though Clipchamp is a fairly basic app, you will most likely come across a situation where you might get stuck trying to figure out how to do something or wonder why you are not getting the results you are expecting.

There are many ways to get help on your project so you should be able to find the information you need with a little bit of searching. You can do things such as read a book (like this one), watch YouTube videos, search the internet or even use the built in Clipchamp help feature. To access the Clipchamp help, simply click on the question mark icon in the editor as seen in figure 5.26.

Figure 5.26

This will open the Clipchamp help options where you can do things such as send them a message with your question. How long it takes to get a reply will vary on whether you have a free account or a paid account. I wouldn't rely on this method 100% because there is no guarantee that you will even get a reply.

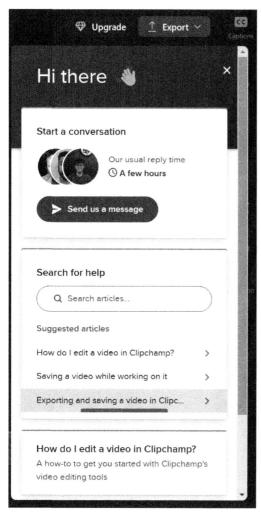

Figure 5.27

You can also search the help articles by typing in your question in the search box. As you type, you will instantly see results related to your search (figure 5.28). You will also be shown random articles or suggested reading at the bottom of the search window as seen in figure 5.27.

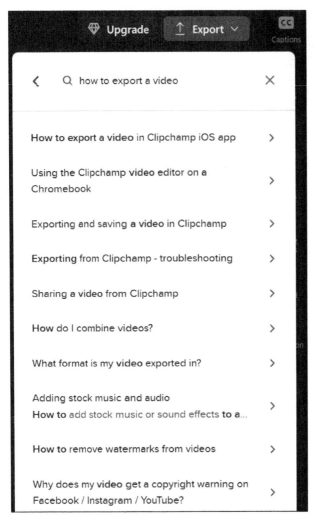

Figure 5.28

What's Next?

Now that you have read through this book and taken your video editing skills to the next level, you might be wondering what you should do next. Well, that depends on where you want to go. Are you happy with what you have learned, or do you want to further your knowledge with more advanced video editing software to try to see if you can make some even more professional looking movies?

If you do want to expand your knowledge, then you can look for some more advanced books such as my book titled **Premiere Elements Made Easy**, if that's the path you choose to follow. Focus on mastering the basics, and then apply what you have learned when going to more advanced material.

There are many great video resources as well, such as Pluralsight or CBT Nuggets, which offer online subscriptions to training videos of every type imaginable. YouTube is also a great source for instructional videos if you know what to search for.

If you are content with being a proficient Clipchamp user that knows more than your friends, then just keep on practicing what you have learned. Don't be afraid to poke around with some of the features that you normally don't use and see if you can figure out what they do without having to research it since learning by doing is the most effective method to gain new skills.

Thanks for reading **Clipchamp Video Editor Made Easy**. You can also check out the other books in the Made Easy series for additional computer related information and training. You can get more information on my other books on my Computers Made Easy Book Series website.

https://www.madeeasybookseries.com/

You should also check out my computer tips website, as well as follow it on Facebook to find more information on all kinds of computer topics.

www.onlinecomputertips.com
https://www.facebook.com/OnlineComputerTips/

About the Author

James Bernstein has been working with various companies in the IT field for over 20 years, managing technologies such as SAN and NAS storage, VMware, backups, Windows Servers, Active Directory, DNS, DHCP, Networking, Microsoft Office, Photoshop, Premiere, Exchange, and more.

He has obtained certifications from Microsoft, VMware, CompTIA, ShoreTel, and SNIA, and continues to strive to learn new technologies to further his knowledge on a variety of subjects.

He is also the founder of the website onlinecomputertips.com, which offers its readers valuable information on topics such as Windows, networking, hardware, software, and troubleshooting. James writes much of the content himself and adds new content on a regular basis. The site was started in 2005 and is still going strong today.

Printed in Great Britain
by Amazon

39417803R00057